Bibliographic information published by the German National Library:

The German National Library lists this publication in the National Bibliography; detailed bibliographic data are available on the Internet at http://dnb.dnb.de .

Imprint:

Copyright © 2019 GRIN Verlag
Print and binding: Books on Demand GmbH, Norderstedt Germany
ISBN: 9783346078841

This book at GRIN:

https://www.grin.com/document/510893

Carolina Gerwin

EU Law. Direct and Indirect Effect

GRIN Verlag

GRIN - Your knowledge has value

Since its foundation in 1998, GRIN has specialized in publishing academic texts by students, college teachers and other academics as e-book and printed book. The website www.grin.com is an ideal platform for presenting term papers, final papers, scientific essays, dissertations and specialist books.

Visit us on the internet:

http://www.grin.com/

http://www.facebook.com/grincom

http://www.twitter.com/grin_com

EU Law: Direct and Indirect Effect

Carolina Gerwin

European Union law is mostly "applied and enforced in a decentralised fashion by national authorities" in the Member States (Reinisch 2012, 58). In this regard, the Court of the European Union (CJEU) has enhanced the effectiveness of EU law by expanding the concept of direct effect to primary sources such as Treaty provisions and to secondary origins of EU law such as regulations and, in exceptions, to directives (Reinisch 2012, 58). Further, the concept of indirect effect is crucial as according to Drake, since the concept creation by the CJEU in the case of *Von Colson* in 1986, "the Court's case law clearly illustrates that 'indirect effect' has played a key role in protecting citizens' rights, particularly in the absence of the horizontal direct effect of Directives" (2005, 1). While I agree that the concept of indirect effect is important for safeguarding individual's rights due to its several beneficial characteristics, recent case law indicates that the principle of horizontal direct effect becomes significantly more important.

The essay starts by focusing on the direct effect of primary EU law, particularly Treaty Articles, before discussing the principle regarding secondary sources, especially directives. After that, strategies developed by the CJEU to neutralise the impact of the rule that directives do not have horizontal direct effect are debated, leading to the conclusion that indirect effect becomes less important.

Although fifty years have passed since its introduction, the doctrine of direct effect is still seen as an *"unwritten principle() of law"* as it is neither codified in EU treaties nor in the constitutions of the Member States (Witte 2011, 347). However, it is accepted everywhere with only few exceptions (Witte 2011, 361).

The CJEU defined direct effect as the "creation of *rights* for individuals" that national courts must protect" (Witte 2011, 330). This is the narrower and "'subjective'" definition of the term (Craig and de Búrca 2015, 186). However, there is a second definition since while many norms of EU law that do not have the creation of rights for individuals as a goal, they are still a useful tool for supervising the actions of Member States (Witte 2011, 330). Therefore, nowadays, according to the broader and "'objective'" definition, direct effect signifies that binding provisions of EU law which are "sufficiently clear, precise, and unconditional to be considered justiciable *can be invoked and relied on* by individuals before national courts" (Craig and de Búrca 2015, 184-86).

Two main reasons for developing direct effect were the securing effectiveness of EU law within Member States, and the consistent application of Union law (Dougan 2011, 409). Furthermore, by giving individuals the possibility of challenging state actions for violating EU law through the concept of direct effect, allowing the *private enforcement* of EU law, individuals became part of the legal order of the EU (Craig and de Búrca 2015, 185). Therefore, due to the judicial creation of direct effect by the CJEU in the 1963, a 'new legal order of international law' has been established that puts the individual and the protection of citizen's rights in the centre (Witte 2011, 358), permitting the domestic enforcement of international law by citizens (Craig and de Búrca 2015, 185). The creation reflects the CJEU's *"vision of the kind of legal community that the Treaties seemed designed to create"*, namely a Community of peoples with individuals at the centre of the system who could obtain rights from the EEC Treaty (Craig and de Búrca 2015, 189). Consequently, the concept of direct effect is the result of the teleological interpretation of the Treaty, where, as opposed to a literal interpretation, the text is interpreted in the meaning of the goal of the Treaty, namely the establishment of a community as described above (Craig and de Búrca 2015, 189).

Regarding the application of the principle of direct effect, the doctrine pertains generally to "all binding EU law including the Treaties, the Charter of the Fundamental Rights, general principles, secondary legislation, and international agreements" (Craig and de Búrca 2015, 184). In terms of primary sources of EU law, namely the EU Treaties and the Charter, this paper focuses on the first one. The reason for this is that in 1963 in the famous *Van Gen den Loos* Case, Case 26/62 NV *Algemene Transporten Expeditie Onderneming van Gend en Loos v Nederlandse Administratie der Belastingen* (1963) ECR 1, the CJEU expressed the doctrine of direct effect for the first time by stating that Treaty Article 12 of the EEC Treaty is directly effective, constituting the "most famous of all its rulings" (Craig and de Búrca 2015, 187). The case was about a Dutch company that imported chemicals from Germany into the Netherlands and stated that Dutch tax authorities applied supposedly increased custom duties on its products contrary to Art. 12 of the EEC Treaty (now Art. 30 TFEU) (Craig and de Búrca 2015, 187). This case is an example of *vertical* direct effect as Van Gend en Loos as an individual challenged a public authority of the Dutch state. The Court laid down the principle of direct effect by stating that the EEC establishes a "new legal order of international law" that has as its subjects not only the Member States but also individuals, not only imposing obligations but also conferring rights upon individuals "which become part of their legal heritage" (European Union a). These utterances imply that direct effect of EU law is an "inherent characteristic" of Community law (Reinisch 2012, 59). This is supported by the fact that the formulation of the doctrine is not only addressed at the Dutch tax authority but at all courts in all EU Member States (Witte 2011, 326). And in this specific case, the Court ruled that because it contains a "clear and unconditional prohibition", Art. 12 "is ideally adapted to produce direct effects in the legal relationship between Member States and their subjects" (European Union a), confirming that the Article is directly effective in a vertical case. The CJEU concluded that due to the "spirit, the general scheme and the wording of the Treaty, Article 12 must be interpreted as producing direct effects and creating individual rights which national courts must protect" (European Union a).

Furthermore, Treaty Articles are also horizontally effective, meaning that an individual can use them to challenge a private party (Craig and de Búrca 2015, 192). Case 43/75 *Defrenne v Sabena* (1956) ECR 455 plays a major role in this development (Mol 2011, 114). The case centred on the former Article 19 EC, now Art. 157 TFEU, as the argument of Defrenne against her private employer regarding discrimination of payment, in comparison with male employee, was based on this Treaty Article (Mol 2011, 114). The CJEU ruled that the "principle that men and women should receive equal pay, which is laid down in Article 119, is one of the foundations of the Community", that one may rely on it before a national court, and that all courts have the duty to protect the rights that individuals attain through that provision (European Union b). Paragraph 10 and 12 of the CJEU's judgement stress that the provision forms a "social objective of the community", serving both an economic and social aim (European Union b), confirming that this case is an "outstanding example of teleological interpretation guided by the *effet utile* of Union law" (Reinisch 2012, 62). The CJEU ruled that as the equal pay principle is mandatory, the prohibition on discrimination is not only applicable to public authorities but also "extends to (…) contracts between individuals" and that courts must protect the rights that the principle of equal pay, contained in Art. 12, grants, also "in cases in which men and women receive unequal pay for equal work which is carried out in the same establishment or service, whether private or public" (European Union b). This shows that Treaty Articles have horizontal direct effect.

Besides the general conditions of direct effect, the "formal *source of law* in which the EU law norm is contained" also plays a role regarding whether a provision is directly effective (Witte 2011, 333). In Art. 288 TFEU, the EU laid down the secondary sources of EU law, namely regulations, directives, decisions, recommendations and opinions (Mittwoch 2013, 13). While regulations and decisions have direct effect, the matter is different regarding directives (Craig and de Búrca 2015, 200). This becomes clear looking at the definition of directives: They are addressed at Member States, they are "binding as to the end to be achieved" and, they leave the method of achieving the aim to the Member States (Craig and de Búrca 2015, 108). Moreover, a directive must be correctly implemented by the EU states within the prescribed time limit (Dougan 2011, 413). Although directives therefore may not always fulfil the three conditions for direct effect (clarity, precision, and unconditionality), the CJEU

3

still decided that directives can be directly effective (Craig and de Búrca 2015, 201). However, as will be shown later, the case law of the CJEU regarding directives faces a tension between two goals: The aim of ensuring the effectiveness of EU law and its uniform application among Member States, and upholding the "specific identity of Directives as a form of indirect legislation" (Dashwood 2006/07, 82).

The reasons for the direct effect of directives were outlined in Case 41/74 *Van Duyn v Home Office* (1973) ECR 1337, and in Case 148/78 *Pubblico Ministero v Tullio Ratti* (1979) ECR 1629 (Craig and de Búrca 2015, 201). In the first case, concerning a Dutch woman who was not allowed to enter the UK as she planned to work for the Church of Scientology that was seen as "'socially harmful'" (Reinisch 2012, 65), the Court stated that *"where the Community authorities have, by directives, imposed on Member States the obligation to pursue a particular course of conduct, the useful effect of such an act would be weakened it individuals were prevented from relying on it before national courts and if the latter were prevented from taking it into consideration as an element of Community law"* (European Union c). Therefore, the first reason concerns the enhanced effectiveness of EU law through private enforcement (Craig and de Búrca 2015, 201). The second cause for direct effect of directives is based on Art. 177, now Art. 267 TFEU, which allows the referral of questions from national courts to the EU, implying that such acts have direct effect (Craig and de Búrca 2015, 201). Especially the first argument shows that the goal of effectiveness of EU law is uppermost in this argumentation (Dashwood 2006/07, 85).

The "'specific identity objective'" was supplied by the Court's judgement in the *Ratti* case (Dashwood 2006/07, 85). In this case, the direct effect of directives worked as a "'shield'" as an Italian national used the labelling provisions of two directives which had not been implemented within the time limit in Italy against his prosecution under the stricter Italian law (Reinisch 2012, 65). The CJEU ruled that "a Member State which has not adopted the implementing measures required by the directive in the prescribed periods may not rely, as against individuals, on its own failure to perform the obligations which the directive entails" (European Union d). This is the estoppel argument (Dashwood 2006/07, 86). This judgement combines two rationales: Ensuring the effectiveness of the directive and "preventing the Member State concerned from gaining a legal advantage through its own default" (Dashwood 2006/07, 86).

However, it is essential to note that the cases above are examples of *vertical* direct effect because in the *Marshall* Case of 1986, the CJEU has determined that directives are not horizontally effective (Craig and de Búrca 2015, 204). In Case 152/84 *Marshall v Southampton and South-West Hampshire*

4

Area Health Authority (Teaching) (1986) ECR 723, Helen Marshall got laid off by a health authority after 14 years' employment as she had passed 60 and the policies of the health authority required female workers to retire at 60, while the age for male employees was 65 (Craig and de Búrca 2015, 204). Consequently, Marshall proceeded against her dismissal by stating that it violated the 1976 Equal Treatment Directive (Craig and de Búrca 2015, 204). However, answering the question whether Marshall could rely on this directive, the Court stated that "the binding nature of a directive (…) exists only in relation to 'each Member State to which it is addressed'" and "that a provision of a directive may not be relied upon as such against such a person" (European Union e). Horizontal direct effect of directives is therefore enunciated.

Nevertheless, the CJEU has introduced alternative strategies for reducing the consequences of the lack of horizontal direct effect of directives (Craig and de Búrca 2015, 206) and the Court further ruled in paragraph 49 that "where a person involved in legal proceedings is able to rely on a directive as against the state he may do so regardless of the capacity in which the latter is acting, whether employer or public authority. In either case it is necessary to prevent the state from taking advantage of its own failure to comply with Community law" (European Union e). This and to secure the effectiveness of EU law, the Court applied one of the six strategies that have been developed by the CJEU (Craig and de Búrca 2015, 206), namely the emanation of the concept of the 'state'. Consequently, since the health authority was a public authority, "Ms Marshall's reliance on Directive 76/207 against it could be regarded as an instance of vertical direct effect" (Dashwood 2006/07, 87).

The idea of this strategy is that for appealing on the vertical direct effect of directives, the definition of the 'state' is expanded, consequently also applying to public employers and private ones with special rights, such as nationalised industries, local authorities, etc. that can be understood as organs of the state (Craig and de Búrca 2015, 206-07). The leading case in this aspect is Case C-188/89 *Foster and Others v British Gas plc* (1990) ECR I-3313 (Craig and de Búrca 2015, 206). The litigators were employees at British Gas that was a nationalised industry and whose policy determined that women were requested to retire at 60 and men at 65 (Craig and de Búrca 2015, 206). Regarding the question whether the plaintiffs could rely on the 1976 Equal Treatment Directive (Craig and de Búrca 2015, 206), the Court decided: "Unconditional and sufficiently precise provisions of a directive may be relied upon against organizations or bodies which are subject to the authority or control of the State or have special powers beyond those which result from the normal rules applicable in relations between individuals" (European Union f). Consequently, the emanation of the concept of the state was the first strategy developed to "neutralise the no horizontal direct effect rule" while maintaining both the effectiveness and special features of directives (Dashwood 2006/07, 90).

The second strategy, namely the concept of indirect effect whose importance is stressed by Drake (2005, 1), was firstly defined in 1984 in the cases of *Von Colson* and *Harz*, when the Court faced the question of how to ensure that the plaintiffs "derived the full benefit of their substantive right to equal treatment notwithstanding the absence of direct effect" of the relevant provisions of the directive (Drake 2005, 1-2). Consequently, the CJEU developed the concept of indirect effect (Drake 2005, 2). This concept, also called the "principle of harmonious interpretation", demands the interpretation of national law in accord with directives (Craig and de Búrca 2015, 209). In Case 14/83 *Von Colson and Kamann v Land Nordrhein-Westfalen* (1984) ECR 1891, concerning the Equal Treatment Directive that the claimants based their prosecution of unlawful sex discrimination on (Craig and de Búrca 2015, 209), the CJEU stated that because Member States have the obligation to achieve the results entailed in the directive, national courts have the obligation to "interpret its national law in the light of the wording and the purpose of the directive" (European Union g).

The rationale behind the concept of indirect effect is not only increasing the effectiveness of EU law, but also the commitment in Article 4(3) TEU (Craig and de Búrca 2015, 210). This paragraph says that based on the principle of sincere cooperation, Member States have the (positive) obligation of taking any appropriate action to secure the achievement of obligations imposed on them by the Treaties or actions of EU institutions, as well as the (negative) obligation to "refrain from any measure which could jeopardise the attainment of the Union's objectives" (European Union h).

One of the advantages of the doctrine of indirect effect is that it also applies in horizontal cases (Drake 2005, 5). This can be seen in Case 212/04 *Konstantinos Adeneler and Others v Ellinikos Organismos Galaktos (ELOG)* (2006) ECR I-6057, as the CJEU emphasized in paragraph 113 of the judgements on the one hand the lack of horizontal direct effect of directives, but states on the other hand that Member States have an obligation to interpret national law in conformity with EU law, which is per definition indirect effect, particularly where a directive lacks direct effect due to the fact that it concerns a horizontal dispute (European Union i).This confirms that horizontal *indirect* effect is possible.
The second advantage of indirect effect is that while direct effect is dependent on the conditions that the provisions of the directive are clear, precise and unconditional, the principle of indirect effect has no such dependencies (Craig and de Búrca 2015, 210).

However, the judgement in the *Adeneler* case also illustrates one of the limits of the doctrine of indirect effect, namely the time limit as the CJEU ruled in paragraph 115 that where the transposition of a directive is delayed, national courts have to interpret national in accord with the directive only once the transition period has expired (European Union i).

Moreover, in Case 80/86 *Kolpinghuis Nijmegen* (1987) ECR 3969, the CJEU claimed that the obligation to interpret national law in accordance with EU law "is limited by the general principles of law which form part of Community law and in particular the principles of legal certainty and non-retroactivity. Therefore a directive cannot, of itself and independently of a national law adopted by a Member State for its implementation, have the effect of determining or aggravating the liability in criminal law of persons who act in contravention of the provisions of that directive" (European Union j).

In the past, as seen above, the CJEU solved the problem of claiming rights conferred on individuals via directives in horizontal disputes, which is essential as directives have a big influence on everyday life of EU citizens, by creating the concept of indirect effect that is also applicable in horizontal cases. Therefore, Drake is right when she stated in 2005 that indirect effect is a pivotal measure for protecting citizen's rights (1). However, recent case law of the CJEU suggest a "horizontalisation" of EU law as the private enforcement of Community law takes mostly part in horizontal rather than vertical cases (Wilman 2015, 559). The Court has and is still increasing the possibilities for the enforcement of EU law by private parties, consequently "transposing and giving further effect to the principle of horizontal direct effect in the procedural and remedial sphere" (Wilman 2015, 559). This is because the CJEU has developed two more strategies to neutralise the impact of the *Marshall* ruling that directives do not have horizontal direct effect, namely the "doctrine of 'incidental horizontal effects'" and the "interaction between general principles and directives" (Craig and de Búrca 2015, 206).

Regarding the first, already in 2001, Tridimas argued on examples such as the *CIA* and *Unilever* cases that provisions of unimplemented directives could be relied upon to put aside incompatible national law (exclusion effect) in cases against another individual (353). In the *CIA* case, for example, the CJEU ruled that "Articles 8 and 9 of Directive 83/189 (…) are to be interpreted as meaning that individuals may rely on them before the national court, which must decline to apply a national technical regulation which has not been notified in accordance with the directive" (European Union k). Consequently, directives can be horizontally effective without directly imposing legal obligations on individual persons by setting aside conflicting national measures, resulting in a disadvantage or a legal liability for one party to which it would not have been subject to if the incompatible national law had been exercised (Craig and de Búrca 2015, 216). Therefore, while the CJEU has promoted its rule that directives do not have direct effect, the Court "permits, if not encourages, its erosion"

(Tridimas 2001, 353) as cases such as *CIA* and *Unilever* show that directives "can be enforced horizontally between the parties, provided that this can be rationalized in terms of an exclusionary (…) effect" (Craig and de Búrca 2015, 219).

Regarding the interaction between a directive and a general principle of law, the doctrine says that citizens can invoke the general principles of EU law to put aside incompatible provisions of national law, even in horizontal cases (Craig and de Búrca 2015, 220). That this is also the case concerning a provision of a directive was confirmed by the *Mangold* case: Although the transposition period of the Framework Employment Directive 2000/78 had not yet expired and the case concerned a private dispute, the litigator "could rely directly on the EU general principle against age discrimination" to protest against the provisions of a fixed-term contract determined by the employer (Craig and de Búrca 2015, 220). The CJEU explained its decision by claiming that national courts have the duty to ensure the success of the principle of non-discrimination based on age and therefore have to set aside contradicting national law even when the time limit has not yet expired, thereby giving horizontal direct effect to the forbiddance of age discrimination (Mol 2011, 118). The CJEU ruled further in paragraph 74 and 75 that it is not the directive itself that is directly effective but rather the principle of non-discrimination due to age that has to be seen as a "general principle of Community law" (European Union l). Consequently, national courts have the responsibility to give supremacy to EU law and to set aside conflicting provisions of national law (European Union l), therefore having an exclusionary effect (Mol 2011, 121). Thus, if a directive contains a general principle of EU law, the directive can have horizontal direct effect, even if the transposition period of the provision has not yet expired. In the case of *Kücükdeveci*, the CJEU emphasised again that it is not the directive but rather the general principle of non-discrimination based on age that provokes the horizontal direct effect of the directive (Mol 2011, 119). The consequences of the "*de facto* horizontal exclusion effect of anti-discrimination directives is far-reaching" as it expands to private disputes and the special identity of directives is endangered by reducing the differences between regulations and directives (Mol 2011, 125). These observances confirm Dashwood's statement that the CJEU favours the effectiveness goal of EU law over the objective to preserve the special characteristics of directives (2006/07, 82).

In conclusion, this paper shows that the CJEU has enhanced the effectiveness of EU law by giving individuals the possibility of challenging the state and other individuals via EU law. The concept of direct effect applies to primary sources such as Treaty Articles in both vertical and horizontal cases. Until a few years ago, regarding (for the citizens very important) directives, individuals could only rely on them to challenge states and not individuals. To close this gap, the CJEU constructed the principle of indirect effect that is also applicable in horizontal cases. Therefore, Drake is right in stating that this concept played a major role in the protection of citizens' rights. During the last years, however, the CJEU has applied new strategies that in fact give horizontal direct effect to directives. Consequently, one can expect that in future the significance of the concept of indirect effect will decrease in favour of horizontal direct effect.

Bibliography

Craig, Paul and Gráinne de Búrca. *EU Law: Text, Cases, and Materials*. Oxford: Oxford University Press, 2015.

Dashwood, Alan. "From *Van Duyn* to *Mangold* via *Marshall*: Reducing Direct Effect to Absurdity?" *Cambridge Yearbook of European Legal Studies* 9 (2006-2007): 81-110. https://heinonline-org.ezproxy.leidenuniv.nl:2443/HOL/Page?lname=&public=false&handle=hein.intyb/camyel0009&page=81&collection=intyb#.

Dougan, Michael. "The Vicissitudes of Life at the Coalface: Remedies and Procedures for Enforcing Union Law Before the National Courts." In *The Evolution of EU Law*, edited by Paul Craig and Gráinne de Búrca, 407-438. Oxford: Oxford University Press, 2011. http://web.a.ebscohost.com.ezproxy.leidenuniv.nl:2048/ehost/ebookviewer/ebook/bmxlYmtfXzY5NDE3OV9fQU41?sid=0c9b70c3-67dc-48cf-a629-e8c42e6b889a@sdc-v-sessmgr05&vid=0&format=EB&rid=1.

Drake, Sara. "Twenty years after Von Colson: the impact of "indirect effect" on the protection of the individual's community rights." *European Law Review*, Vol. 30(3) (June 2005): 1-16. https://login-westlaw-co-uk.ezproxy.leidenuniv.nl:2443/maf/wluk/app/document?access-method=toc&src=toce&docguid=IB9FDB580E72111DA9D198AF4F85CA028&crumb-action=append&context=3.

European Union a. "Judgment of the Court of 5 February 1963." Accessed December 28, 2018. https://eur-lex.europa.eu/legal-content/EN/TXT/?uri=CELEX%3A61962CJ0026.

European Union b. "Judgment of the Court of 8 April 1976." Accessed December 28, 2018. https://eur-lex.europa.eu/legal-content/EN/TXT/?uri=CELEX%3A61975CJ0043.

European Union c. "Judgment of the Court of 4 December 1974." Accessed December 29, 2018. https://eur-lex.europa.eu/legal-content/EN/TXT/?uri=CELEX%3A61974CJ0041.

European Union d. "Judgment of the Court of 5 April 1979." Accessed December 29, 2018. https://eur-lex.europa.eu/legal-content/EN/TXT/?uri=CELEX%3A61978CJ0148.

European Union e. "Judgment of the Court of 26 February 1986." Accessed December 29, 2018. https://eur-lex.europa.eu/legal-content/EN/TXT/?uri=CELEX%3A61984CJ0152.

European Union f. "Judgment of the Court of 12 July 1990." Accessed December 30, 2018. https://eur-lex.europa.eu/legal-content/EN/TXT/?uri=CELEX%3A61989CJ0188.

European Union g. "Judgment of the Court of 10 April 1984." Accessed December 30, 2018. https://eur-lex.europa.eu/legal-content/EN/TXT/?uri=CELEX%3A61983CJ0014.

European Union h. "Consolidated version of the Treaty on European Union - TITLE I COMMON PROVISIONS - Article 4." Accessed December 30, 2018. https://eur-lex.europa.eu/legal-content/EN/TXT/?uri=CELEX%3A12012M004.

European Union i. "Judgment of the Court (Grand Chamber) of 4 July 2006." Accessed December 30, 2018. https://eur-lex.europa.eu/legal-content/GA/TXT/?uri=CELEX:62004CJ0212.

European Union j. "Judgment of the Court (Sixth Chamber) of 8 October 1987." Accessed December 30, 2018. https://eur-lex.europa.eu/legal-content/EN/TXT/?uri=CELEX%3A61986CJ0080.

European Union k. "Judgment of the Court of 30 April 1996." Accessed January 2, 2019. https://eur-lex.europa.eu/legal-content/GA/TXT/?uri=CELEX:61994CJ0194.

European Union l. "Judgment of the Court (Grand Chamber) of 22 November 2005." Accessed January 2, 2019. https://eur-lex.europa.eu/legal-content/EN/TXT/?uri=CELEX%3A62004CJ0144.

Mittwoch, Anne-Christin. *Vollharmonisierung und Europäisches Privatrecht: Methode, Implikationen und Durchführung*. Berlin/ Boston: Walter de Gruyter GmbH, 2013. https://www-degruyter-com.libproxy.ucl.ac.uk/viewbooktoc/product/207440.

Mol, Mirjam de. "The Novel Approach of the CJEU on the Horizontal Direct Effect of the EU Principle of Non-Discrimination: (Unbridled) Expansionism of EU Law?" *Maastricht Journal of European and Comparative Law* 18, no. 1–2 (March 2011): 109–35. https://journals-sagepub-com.ezproxy.leidenuniv.nl:2443/doi/abs/10.1177/1023263X1101800106#articleCitationDownloadContainer.

Reinisch, August. *Essentials of EU Law*. Cambridge: Cambridge University Press, 2012. https://www-cambridge-org.libproxy.ucl.ac.uk/core/books/essentials-of-eu-law/2C34E28A9F7A5367E0269538B50672AE.

Tridimas, Takis. "Black, White, and Shades of Grey: Horizontality of Directives Revisited." *Yearbook of European Law*, Vol. 21(1) (2001): 327-354. https://search-proquest-com.libproxy.ucl.ac.uk/docview/1564197523?rfr_id=info%3Axri%2Fsid%3Aprimo.

Wilman, Folkert. *Private Enforcement of EU Law Before National Courts: The EU Legislative Framework*. Cheltenham and Northampton: Edward Elgar Publishing, 2015. https://www-elgaronline-com.libproxy.ucl.ac.uk/view/9781784718480.xml.

Witte, Bruno de. „ Direct Effect, Primacy, and the Nature of the Legal Order." In *The Evolution of EU Law*, edited by Paul Craig and Gráinne de Búrca, 323-362. Oxford: Oxford University Press, 2011. http://web.a.ebscohost.com.ezproxy.leidenuniv.nl:2048/ehost/ebookviewer/ebook/bmxlYmtfXzY5NDE3OV9fQU41?sid=0c9b70c3-67dc-48cf-a629-e8c42e6b889a@sdc-v-sessmgr05&vid=0&format=EB&rid=1.

YOUR KNOWLEDGE HAS VALUE

- We will publish your bachelor's and master's thesis, essays and papers

- Your own eBook and book - sold worldwide in all relevant shops

- Earn money with each sale

Upload your text at www.GRIN.com
and publish for free